*Sit, Walk, and Stand
in Every Heavenly Blessing*

Vivien
thank you
& love
Blessing
Troy

Sit, Walk, and Stand in Every Heavenly Blessing

Inspired by the Book of Ephesians

LaTanya Mack *and*
Kenya Wallace Williams

To order additional copies of this book, contact:
Xlibris Corporation
1-888-795-4274
www.Xlibris.com
Orders@Xlibris.com
107490

Contents

DEDICATIONS:

This book is dedicated in loving memory of

Hellon Maxie (Mom)
Catherine Hubbard (Sister)

Who always assisted and encouraged me in all of my many endeavors. They also taught me how to stand in Christ Jesus and never lose sight of my goals.
I am ever grateful for their love, teaching and many blessings.

Diane and Vieda Thanks' for understanding, praying and encouraging me everyday. You are my sisters, my daughters and my friends. Praise God!

John, Kenya, BJ, and TJ: It is about you. Thanks for always sharing. You are a blessing. I love you more,

My Sweet, Sweet Darlings!

La Tanya's
ACKNOWLEDGEMENTS:

I thank my Heavenly Father who is the Lord of the harvest for sending laborers into my life to plant and water fruitful seeds. And I enjoy the work of The Holy Spirit always in the world. So much work, so many fields, so many seasons, and one God.

Thanks to my siblings who always understand and cover me when I fall short of my obligations. I am ever grateful for your love. Favor is not fair, but it's yours.

For My People family, Pastor Patterson (Ida); Pastor Parker (Brenda) Ms Hattie; Ms Crystal; the Ross family; and each member, thanks for praying for and believing in me even in difficult times. Lord, bless them all, really good.

Beulah, you are an inspiration in so many ways my friend. I like your style. Always reaching, always teaching: wise woman of God. Lord, keep her in perfect peace.

Val, Juanita and Mary, my friends and co-laborers with so much energy, who went the extra mile to complete this project, I love you.

Thank you my Cathedral family, and especially Pastor Charles (Tammi) and Pastor Lynn for your time, teaching and prayers. Bishop and Norma Paulk; Pastors Don (Clarice)Paulk; also Pastors DE (Brandi) Paulk and all of the excellent leadership at Chapel Hill. Thanks for speaking the new sound of Christ Consciousness into the kingdom; Lord sees faithful fore-runners.

A special thanks to all of Grannies' Sweet Darlings who believed in me and in turn prayed with or inspired me in any way to compile utterances from conversations with My Lord to book form. It has been a journey, Thanks for staying with me. God gets all the Glory Forever and ever.

Mieka, Scott& Deanna: Smooches
Eltony, Curtiss, Albert, Dave and Rob: Thanks for being You

I love you all.

Kenya's
ACKNOWLEDGEMENTS

I thank you awesome God for life, love and a willingness to always seek truth. You love me and keep me even in my wrong choices, merciful and faithful God. You sent Grandmother to show me everyday is a good day because it is God's day. Thanks for her too.

Also, I am grateful for my parents and siblings, BJ and TJ: we are a circle of friends. I love you and appreciate all that you do. Hugs and kisses.

Aunt Diane and Aunt Denise, I appreciate your advice so much. You are my angels.

Robert Kelly, I remember everything: I wish showers of blessings continue to flow in your life---thanks.

Many thanks to my fusion family: Especially Pastor Cassius (Heather), K.O, Maggie and Joe: You are the best.

Thanks Sean for being there time after time.

And, heartfelt thanks to all my family and friends not mentioned by name. I am ever blessed by our journey together. I love you all and I pray our future will be greater than our past.

Foreword

Pro-Love,
Here it is.

Inspiration comes in many forms. From the ultimate Word made flesh, Jesus, the Christ, to the written prose and poetry of ancient sacred texts, God speaks to His creation through H is creation. In this particular book, LaTanya Mack and Kenya has allowed God's love and creativity to flow through them in the form of beautiful poems of comfort, worship, guidance and most of all love. I hope each and every reader will be as inspired by them as I have been.

Senior Pastor D.E. Paulk
Cathedral of The Holy Spirit
Decatur, Ga

Introduction

Deposits

1ˢᵗ Corinthians 3:6-7 NKJV

I have planted, Apollo's watered; but God gave the increase.
So then neither is he that planted any thing, neither he that watered;
But God that gives the increase.

Reveal more than rhyming words my Lord:

Awaken
Words of comfort and protection
Words of deliverance and praise
Words of hope and direction
Restoring confidence, always

Living words that spark life
And incite a desire to be free
Words of truth, piercing darkness
With holy boldness and authority

Release
Skilled Watchmen who inspire to and fro
Releasing love deposits where living waters flow
Proclaim the Good-news; we are predestined for a reason
Holy Spirit yield a harvest for the kingdom in due-season

Amen!!!

This is our sincere prayer for each word written in this book.
Tanya & Kenya

A New Sound

Acts 2:2 NIV

**Suddenly a sound like the blowing of a violent wind came from heaven
And filled the whole house where they were sitting.**

*A new sound
Renewed hope
A new day*

*Healed spirit
Willing heart
To pray,
Today-today*

*I've entered thru that open door
Seeking You Lord, like never before
Tearing down walls, please restore
Love and peace forevermore
Today-today*

*A new sound
Renewed hope
A new day*

*Healed spirit
Willing heart
To pray,
Today-today*

I'm thirsting for truth as I watch and pray
To hear what The Spirit has to say
I submit Lord, have your way
Break forth new sounds into the world
Today-today

A new sound
Renewed hope
A new day
Jesus-Jesus

Healed spirit
Willing heart
To pray,
Today-today

All Come

Revelation 21:3 NIV

**And I heard a loud voice from the throne saying,
"Now the dwelling of God is with men,
He will live with them. They will be his people,
and God himself will be with them and be their God."**

*You make it all possible
You make it all possible
You make it all possible
You make it all worthwhile*

*Knowing You Love Me
Knowing You Keep Me
Knowing You Guide Me
Because I am Your Child*

*I didn't know what to do
With all I was going through
Then I looked and saw You
With Loving outstretched Hands*

Come, Yield and Trust You
Use the keys to make it thru
Lamb's Tree of Life who
Empowers' me to stand

Reveal Your Plan for Me
Awaken me to possibilities
Everything's an opportunity
To heed Your Loving Call

You are Alpha and Omega
Creator of the Universe
You are The Great-I Am
And Master of It All

Amen

Romans 12:2 NIV

Do not conform to the pattern of this world, but be transformed by the renewing of your mind. Then you will be able to test and approve what God's will is—his good, pleasing and perfect will.

Tell me, how I can say-Amen
The tormentor's already back again
He says I'm a failure as a man
Amen means I've got finality
I really do want to be free
But those thoughts keep worrying me

Don't listen-don't listen

Trying hard to hold on tight
Toss and turn in confusion all night
Wrestle all day to do what's right

Now Listen

I see the tears streaming down your face
Just keep the faith, even at that pace
The Lord will help you win the race
Take one minute and hour at a time
Jesus promises, "you will be just fine
Not your battle-this one's mine"

Now listen-just listen

Jesus loves you 24 hours a day
He's with you, even when you stray
Rest in His arms Beloved: It's ok
His blood covers you, anyway
Just trust Him when you pray
Come-on now, let me hear you say

Doubt, "You get out of my way
I'm not listening, and I can finally say
You're defeated, as of today"

Ancient of Days

Daniel 7: 13-14 NIV

"In my vision at night I looked, and there before me was one like a son of man, coming with the clouds of heaven. He approached the Ancient of Days and was led into his presence. He was given authority, glory and sovereign power; all peoples, nations and men of every language worshiped him. His dominion is an everlasting dominion that will not pass away, and his kingdom is one that will never be destroyed."

God of hope, God of praise
Ever loving, Ancient of Days

God of vision and purpose too
Every word, you spoke is true

Every promise and every phrase
Ever loving, Ancient of Days

You know all we say and do
El, we're nothing without you

Out of dust you formed man
With a perfect-masterful plan

Named and called, before birth
To take dominion of the earth

Highly favored with authority
Walk by the Spirit, not what we see

Subdue, posses and occupy the land
Guide us with Your Righteous Hand

Almighty God-Great and true
All our hope rests in You

Almighty God, worthy of praise
Ever faithful, Ancient of Days!

Blessed of The Lord, say so!

John 3:16 NIV

**For God so loved the world that he gave his one and only Son,
that whoever believes in him shall not perish but have eternal life.**

*Thank You for love and every blessing that empowers me
Thanks for canceling all sin, and nailing it on a tree*

*Your truth reveals light in man where sin can no longer hide
Precious Lamb chosen by God, reconcile every soul to Thee*

*We embody grace and mercy, and our life has no end
Your Spirit dwells inside us Lord, to love ourselves again*

*Thanks for this perfect day, I hunger and thirst for truth
Holy boldness of Queen Esther; devotion and faith of Ruth*

*I marvel at all creation, you gave man dominion to keep
I bow humbly before you, remind us what we sow we reap*

And when we fall short of love, please give us a gentle touch
Rescue us from the enemy's hand; Lord we need you so much

No substitute for your blood, shed on the cross at Calvary
Could cancel mans sin before God, and offer complete victory

You paid our debt forever, the veil is torn, and I'm free
Your blood has made it possible, for my God to look at me

Your work on earth is finished; Your Spirit now lives in me
To love All men as brothers Lord, we're related Spiritually

Thanks for each occasion, to walk in forgiveness every day
Seventy times seven for the brethren, is really a small price to pay

Amen!

Climb

Jeremiah 29:11 NIV

For I know the plans I have for you," declares the LORD, "Plans to prosper you and not to harm you, plans to give you hope and a future."

Our journeys path crossed for a reason
And we need each other for this season
Life's purpose shines brighter every hour
Revealing our destiny with amazing power

It doesn't matter who reaches the top first
I'll share my water when you thirst
Let's not push each other away
Love covers' differences—so celebrate

We'll not think about tomorrow, or
Yesterday's heartbreak with its sorrows
Today's Grace is on my mind
God created our journey For the climb

We're together for this reason
To complete each other in this season
Not about position, mistake or trend
Not about being foe or friend
Even though we can't see the journey's end
It's the climb

Not about being friend or foe
It's all about letting go
Surrendering to what we already know
Love is the answer for peace to flow
In the climb

Doesn't matter who's wrong or right
We agreed to be the light
Journeys fixed we've won the fight
Now climb—just climb—with confidence climb!

Focus on what God says': Even when folks manifest that's good,
Celebrate!!! It's your turn because God said so and He is well pleased.

Amen

Come Alive

Acts 2:17 NIV

"'In the last days, God says, I will pour out my Spirit on all people. Your sons and daughters will prophesy, your young men will see visions, your old men will dream dreams.'"

You already live inside of me
Come alive inside of me
You already live inside of me
Today

Come alive inside of me
You already live inside of me
Come alive inside of me
Lord,
I pray

Where can I go that you're not there
What can I do that you don't care
Father, you are everywhere
With Your Love
Your Precious Love

Amen!

Comfort

2 Corinthians 1:3-5 NIV

Praise be to the God and Father of our Lord Jesus Christ, the Father of
compassion and the God of all comfort, who comforts us in all our troubles,
so that we can comfort those in any trouble with the comfort we ourselves
receive from God. For just as we share abundantly in the sufferings of
Christ, so also our comfort abounds through Christ

The Lord's arms are opened wide
He bids the lowly and needy to "come abide"
Leave hurts, anger, fear and pride
All come,
Rest in His love and peace—on the inside

Now and forevermore,

Amen!

Dee and Vee

Micah 6:8 NIV

He has shown you, O mortal, what is good.
And what does the LORD require of you?
To act justly and to love mercy and to walk humbly with your God

Who will love the unloving
Bring them comfort and Peace

Who can speak to the hurts of others
And cause confidence to increase

Who'll hold their hands with a gentle touch
With truth and Love—that means so much

It is you my daughters
My sisters and best friends
Everything we experience
Is for our good, in the end

Your smiling face
And warm embrace
Reach the unloving
In that secret place

Wherever you go
God smiles through you
A rare gift from the Master
Love tried and true

Give God all the credit
Glory, honor and praise
We are already victorious
He blessed all our days!

No matter the battle
Just take a stand
Watch truth prevail
God has your hand

He's food for the journey
And of course
Forever and always
God is your source

Keep sharing your gift
That comes naturally
Follow Grace and Love
Wrapped up in mercy

That warm embrace and gentle touch
Flowing from you really means so much.

Desire

Psalm *37: 4-5 NKJV*

Delight yourself also in the Lord: And He shall give you the desires of your heart. Commit your way to the LORD, Trust also in Him, and He shall bring *it* to pass.

Isaiah 55:10 NIV

As the rain and the snow come down from heaven, and do not return to it without watering the earth and making it bud and flourish, so that it yields seed for the sower and bread for the eater,

Lord Your:
Blessings come to me
To flow through me
And each opportunity
Increases my ability
To be a blessing
More freely

In Jesus Name,

Amen!

Destiny

John 1:48 NIV

"How do you know me?" Nathaniel asked. Jesus answered
"I saw you while you were still under the fig tree before Philip called you.

Hey man, you standing over there
Killing the whole world with your stare
That stocking cap covering your hair
And Glover's mange scent everywhere

I'm talking to you, what's your name
Come on over and don't be shame
Want to shoot marbles: Just one game
Forget the hurts and those you blame

Got Aggies and spinners to share
You can go first, man I don't care
Winner takes all, whatever's fair
Except my cats eye, know that's rare

I see you brought your bag with you
But all your marbles look brand new
Come-on, tell me who messed with you
And I'll get them if you want me too

Friends for a lifetime, with years to go
Thankful for our destiny's flow
So many things we still don't know
Just tend the seeds we're led to sow

God sent you there to help me see
That I had tetter: tetter didn't have me
I kept those marbles purposely
You and marbles helped me break free

Amen!!

Everything

Matthew 27:51 NIV

At that moment the curtain of the temple was torn in two from top to bottom. The earth shook, the rocks split . . .

You are my love and
You are my peace and
You are everything I'm looking for

You are my hope and
You are my source and
You are my Lord Forevermore

Forevermore-Forevermore

That's why I adore and
Honor You my Lord
You're everything I'm looking for
And Awesome God, You're so much more

Forevermore-Forevermore

You make daybreak sing
Guide the eagle's wings
Order the storm to rest
Teach me to do my best
You Love me anyway
Even when I don't obey

You're everything I'm looking for
And Awesome God, You're so much more
You're everything I'm looking for
And Awesome God, You're so much more
The veil is torn, now I can soar
Forevermore-Forevermore

Amen!

Excellent, Is Your Name Lord

Psalm 8:1 NIV

O LORD, our Lord,
How majestic is your name in all the earth!
You have set your glory above the heavens.

Don't know what to do Lord; and I really don't know how
Tried everything else and failed; I am leaning on you now

So many storms arising in my life, everywhere I look
Grant me peace and wisdom, from promises in your book

I am tired of confusion, so I'm asking in Your Mighty Name
Fill me with compassion and hope; remove fear and shame

I need strength to wait in Love, and praise you while I'm in it
To trust and obey Your Spirit Lord, and rest for just a minute

Teach me to pray until time to shout, in triumphant victory
You're all knowing Sovereign Lord; waiting on a call from me

Beloved:
"Out of your loins
Birth greatness
Honor and good fruit
Lacking no good thing
From the stem to the root"

You are mighty in battle Righteous God and keep me in your mind
Thank you for Mercy and Faithfulness; you are with me all the time

I see beyond my present situation; see how to conquer and soar
I'm crowned with glory and honor Lord; I'm not a victim anymore

Oh Lord, our Lord,
How majestic is your name in all the earth . . .

FAITH

John 14: 26-27 NIV

"But the Counselor, the Holy Spirit, whom the Father will send in my name, will teach you all things and will remind you of everything I have said to you. Peace I leave with you; my peace I give you. I do not give to you as the world gives. Do not let your hearts be troubled and do not be afraid."

The Holy Spirit lives in me; He keeps everything all right
He comforts and counsels me, morning, noon and night

As every care, doubt and worry, is flushed outside of me
I'm filled with peace and joy; strong, confident and free

The Holy Spirit anointing breaks yokes every time I pray
Obstacles' are destroyed; and confusion fades away

He helps me walk by faith, prevent fear from stepping in
Thanks for Your Spirit Lord, You sent to be my friend

The Comforter waits to help, all who trust and call
God lives in us by His Spirit, to become our all and all

Increase Your Spirit in us daily, Dear Lord
In Jesus Name,

Amen!

Food for the Journey

Galatians 5:22-26 NIV

But the fruit of the Spirit is love, joy, peace, forbearance, kindness, goodness, faithfulness, gentleness and self-control. Against such things there is no law. Those who belong to Christ Jesus have crucified the flesh with its passions and desires. Since we live by the Spirit, let us keep in step with the Spirit. Let us not become conceited, provoking and envying each other.

Worshippers carry The Ark of Testimony (The presence of The Lord), wherever they go. Worshippers bring and present Jesus to every situation, simply because they are there. Truth in Love exposes lies, (by shining light in darkness and converting hearts). This truth breaks chains and releases captives from bondage. This truth is a gift of Christ Jesus character in the comfort of The Holy Spirit.

Since worshippers are free to share the Love of the Holy Spirit in Truth, my prayer is: Everything that has breath, Praise God!

The Holy Spirit reminds us of our agreement (in the beginning) of our purpose and destiny as we journey. That's why we know when He speaks. We choose to build walls or bridges as we carry out every thought. As we grow and keep in step with the Spirit, the fruit of The Spirit establishes our inner peace in comfort and discernment.

Zacchaeus came expecting and seeking Jesus
Jesus came seeking and Blessing Zacchaeus
Most importantly, Zacchaeus said "yes" and obeyed!
Luke 19:1-10

Amen!

Forever

Psalm *23:1 NIV*

The LORD is my Shepherd, I lack nothing.

Forever sing Your praises, Lord
Forever exalt Your Name
The power you hold today, Lord
Is eternally the same

I'm strengthened and I'm comforted
Each day I walk with Thee
In the Glory of Your presence
Is Righteous Authority

Forever, one day with you Lord
The Kingdom needs Your Grace
Many laborers are interceding
But, not one can take your place

Forever, I will worship
In love and victory
Now, mercy has replaced justice
From bondage I'm set free

Forever sing your praises, Lord
Forever exalt Your Name
Forever grateful you called me, Lord
Forever glad I came . . .

Amen

Forgiven

Luke 23:34 NIV

Jesus said, "Father, forgive them, for they do not know what they are doing."

How can He forgive me for the things I've done
Knowing I've rejected His Love and His Son

FORGIVEN-FORGIVEN-FORGIVEN

What about the spear that pierced His side
Blood and water flowed midst anger and pride
What about the crown of thorns placed on His head
The disgrace and hurt He felt as He bled

FORGIVEN-FORGIVEN-FORGIVEN

What about the mockery He was forced to endure
Am I forgiven for every lie, and made pure
What about the nails driven in His hands and feet
Can I be forgiven for murder and deceit

FORGIVEN-FORGIVEN-FORGIVEN

Jesus hung from the cross and was crucified
Yet He forgave our sins before He died
He rose from the grave, lives in you and me
Ambassadors' of Love with triumphant victory

Transform your mind to Eternal Life
In Christ, the Lamb and Perfect Sacrifice
Open your heart and humbly receive
The truth in Love, and just believe
Grace and mercy is yours to choose
You are Forgiven, now ain't that Good-News
You are Forgiven, now ain't that Good-News

You're never forsaken; you are forgiven and reconciled in
The Precious Blood of Jesus

Forgiven—for every nail, for every lie, for every offense so don't cry
You are forgiven, ain't that good news
Accepted into the family of Love and Grace
Forever,

Amen!

Freedom

Acts 22:28 NIV

**Then the commander said, "I had to pay a big price for my citizenship."
"But I was born a citizen," Paul replied.**

*Lord, I am free
To Honor and bless You Jesus
Lord I am free
To praise Your Holy Name*

*Lord, I am free
To evoke your presence with-in me
Lord I am free
Of Religion and it's shame*

*Lord I am free
Happy to be called a Citizen
Lord I am free
Every limit is removed from me*

*Lord I am free
To love everyone as brothers
Lord I am free
To be a bridge into destiny*

I am finally free
To allow-Your will be done
You created us for this reason
Your Kingdom Family is one

Lord I am free
To serve in grace till you call
Sharing the True Love of Jesus
With all men large and small

I'm free to declare
"Brothers you are already free
Every Sin has been forgiven
Since Christ nailed Sin to the tree."

Friends

Isaiah 40:31 NIV

**But those who hope in the LORD will renew their strength.
They will soar on wings like eagles; they will run and not grow weary,
they will walk and not be faint.**

*It is so hard to soar
When your mind's at war
A ball of confusion
Just one big contusion*

*All out of step
Moving without pep
What are you looking at me like that for
My minds at war*

*You want me to rest
Yet do my best
I really want to do it
Will you help me get through it
I hear what you're saying
And know you're not playing*

*What are you looking at me like that for
I told you, my minds at war-my minds at war*

You say there's nothing to it
That only I can do it
Just rearrange things inside
Release all anger and pride
Admit what I truly need
Holy Spirit sow that seed
Love and Faith will restore
My eagerness to soar
I'll see what's holding me back
And get back on track
I'll get back on track

I've opened my hearts door
I expect so much more
I see how to do my best
My minds healed and at rest
What are you looking at me like that for
Haven't you seen an Eagle Soar
Above the war
Forevermore

Fruits

Titus *3:14 NIV*

Our people must learn to devote themselves to doing what is good,
In order to provide for urgent needs and not live unproductive lives.

Start each day with Thank You Lord
And end each day with the same

Bless everyone you meet with joy
In our Beloved Christ Jesus, name

Sing Songs of Zion with gladness
In the Spirit of Truth and Praise

No weapon formed against you can stand
God's favor on your life, always

You are a Blessing to the Kingdom
Your work has not gone unseen

That special gift of defeating the enemy
With the authority of a queen

The love, life and hope you share
It's only befitting for God to

Honor and take those blessings you give
And place them all on you.

Thank you for all of the visits, prayers and encouragement
That flows through you, wise woman of God!

Lovingly,

In Jesus Precious Name

Give To Receive

1 John *4:10-11 NIV*

**This is love:
Not that we loved God, but that he loved us and sent
his Son as an atoning sacrifice for our sins.
Dear friends, since God so loved us, we also ought to love one another.**

*Familiar faces we see in the neighborhood
Are in agony, in some way, yet not understood*

*The suffering is so deep: it's become a way of life
They cannot see beyond their dependence on strife*

*Their facial expression says "don't bother me, just go away"
The hurts so deep inside: "I've forgotten how to pray"*

*Don't use a chisel or a mallet, to release what they need
Be led by the Holy Spirit, just plant that little seed*

*Water it with love, much encouragement and tender care
God increases the harvest of that sowing beyond compare*

*Your ministry may be one person, just impart what you know
Look beyond faults, help needs and blessings will flow*

Don't look for great signs or miracles, God knows who to send
Often times He heals suffering with a whisper in the wind

Maybe your sister or brothers focus has been misdirected
Prayer, praise and trust in God probably has been neglected

It's up to you, bearer of Good-News, to give your brother facts
"God's spirit in me loves His Spirit in you: brother don't hold back"

So go ahead, trust in God; drink long from your bitter cup
You'll hunger and thirst no more, nor use your blessings up

The most important news for familiar faces to understand
Is that healing and peace comes from God, not from man

My God is able to heal you wherever it hurts

Amen!

God is God

Numbers 23:19 NIV

God is not a man, that he should lie,
Nor a son of man,
that he should change his mind.
Does he speak and then not act?
Does he promise and not fulfill?

God is God and He will not lie
Nor is God afraid

God will accomplish in His own time
Every word that He said

I have to admit I sinned before Him
God was still right there

And when I cried out He answered

Lovingly,

"Have faith child, don't despair."

Amen!

God's Perfect Will

Romans 12:2 NIV

Do not conform any longer to the pattern of this world, but be transformed by the Renewing of your mind. Then you will be able to test and approve what God's will is His good, pleasing and perfect will.

God's perfect will is perfect for you
He loves you, no matter what you do

God's will is perfect without a doubt
His will is perfect, inside and throughout

God's will is perfect, indeed
My God plants the perfect seed

God gathers and scatters as the Trinity chooses
He adds and subtracts—discards or uses

God's thoughts are Holy and will always stay
But every other desire quickly passes away

We can be altered, but His will does not stray
Because He is the potter and we are the clay

God's will is perfect; I tried it, you see
I know it will be perfect for you; it is for me

Selah!

Gen 1:27-28 NIV

So God created man in his own image,
in the image of God he created him;
Male and female he created them.
God blessed them and said to them, "Be fruitful and increase in number;
Fill the earth and subdue it. Rule over the fish of the sea and the birds of the
air and over every living creature that moves on the ground."

You created us for your purpose: By your perfect will
Released us to live in unity: Not to plunder and kill

Why then do we walk by sight: Trusting in what we see
Walking in bondage to temporal things: Thinking that we're free

Who told us we were naked: How did he get in
Exposing us to pain and burden: Revealing death and sin

God's original purpose for man: Forever will be
Take dominion, multiply: Walk in love and harmony

If your hope is built on man and flesh: Come-on and admit it
Get reconciled with God, my friend and Favor along with it

Father has already recorded, every word you've thought and said
You're cleansed and already forgiven, because Jesus Blood was shed

The enemy will come back around and try to keep you company
Don't entertain him, just speak the words: I choose love and unity

The Joy of the Lord is our strength
Amen!

Good Morning Lord

Psalm 31:19-20 NIV

**How abundant are the good things that you have stored up for those who fear
you, which you bestow in the sight of all, on those who take refuge in you.
In the shelter of your presence you hide them from all human intrigues;
You keep them safe in your dwelling from accusing tongues.**

*Good morning Lord
My God and my friend
You are ever present
You are my spirit with-in*

*You know all about me
You Love me anyway
Faithfully guide my spirit
To love and to pray*

*All power and authority
Is in Your mighty hand
Pull down every stronghold
Expose all enemy plans*

*Rescue my spirit, forever
To be committed to You
Seeking to Bless the Kingdom
In all I say and do*

Overtake every attack, Lord
And defeat that enemy
Lord-God Almighty
Love is the spirit that's free

Hallelujah to Your name, Lord
Forever and a day
You're present in your perfect plan
Even when I stray

Amen!

Hands of Mercy

1 Corinthians 3:6 NIV

I planted the seed, Apollo's watered it, but God made it grow.

Hands of Mercy from State to State
Promoting Love, so all can relate

Declaring Peace from Town to Town
Lifting up differences, not tearing them down

Striking the anvil on one accord
Acknowledge One Creator, One God, One Lord

Look past the labels; awaken the Spirit with-in
God loves' all His children, my brother and friend

Whatever the situation, anywhere we may be
Love is: The Power and the opportunity

To share the light, and show mercy
Extend a hand: Confirm all men are free

Grace, mercy, and peace will be with us from God the Father and from Jesus
The Messiah, the Father's Son, in truth and love. 2 John 1:3 AMP

Share the light
Whether dim or bright
Love is—
Always right.

MERCY: Compassion, Forgiveness, kindness, understanding . . .

He Reigns

John 5:6, 8-9 NIV

Jesus saw him lying there and learned that he had been in this condition for a long time, He asked him, "Do you want to get well?" Then Jesus said to him, "Get up! Pick up your mat and walk." At once the man was cured . . .

He reigns, He reigns
His Blessings I proclaim
I'm healed, I'm healed
Healed in Jesus Name

He lives, He lives
And has His hands on me
I'm Anointed with power
And walk in victory

Glory—Hallelujah
I'll never be the same
By faith, my faith
I know that He reigns

No sickness, pain or disease
Has any authority
He reigns, He reigns
And commands Liberty

He reigns, He reigns
His Blessings I proclaim
I'm healed, I'm healed
Healed in Jesus Name

Amen!

Hello Jesus

Psalm 32:1-2 NIV

**Blessed is the one whose transgressions are forgiven, whose sins are covered.
Blessed is the one whose sin the LORD does not count
against them and in whose spirit is no deceit.**

*I feel Your Faithful Presence
Inside me once again
Jesus you're my everything
My Lord and my friend*

*I feel you gently guiding me
Regardless where I go
Spirit of Love says follow Truth
Even when flesh says no*

*Thank You my Lord for Mercy
Each-time you speak to me
Jesus, your blood gave me a choice
To stay bound or break free*

*I know there are times I fail the test
From choices that I make
Thanks for Unconditional Love
You paid for my sake*

You know everything about me
And Love me anyway
The Greatest Intercessor
That helps me when I pray

Even when my choice is wrong
You already understand
That's why we call you Lord and
Everyone else is man

I repent and forgive myself
And walk in your authority
Lean on you in every weakness
My mind can't condemn me

Jesus, you are ever present
Everything you do is blessed
Awesome God, You're ever knowing
And with me in each test!

Hide Or Seek

Hebrews 4:12-13 NIV

For the word of God is living and active. Sharper than any double-edged sword, it penetrates even to dividing soul and spirit, joints and marrow; it judges the thoughts and attitudes of the heart. Nothing in all creation is hidden from God's sight. Everything is uncovered and lay bare before the eyes of him to whom we must give account.

What is my motive
What is my intent
And who really is my source
When my money's spent

Who do I call on
When the road get's tough
When sickness or disaster happens
Frankly, who do I trust

Who do I lean on
Whenever I'm in need
Answer the question truthfully
What's the root of my seed

Upon true evaluation
And self examination
The honest explanation

God,

Sometimes, it's not You!

Higher Dimensions

John 4: 24 *NKJV*

God *is* Spirit and those who worship Him must worship in spirit and truth."

How can you disappoint me: In what I already knew

I know what's in you and I am calling it forth,
Both the wheat and the tare

Flow in the process of Higher Revelation

I am separating and cultivating—feel the chaff burning.

Keep coming forth, I've got you
We agreed in the spirit

The cares of this world have clouded your vision
Awaken and see . . .

Now that you are hearing,
Believe and Be

The Answer!!!

"I Will Separate"

Matthew 13:30 NIV

Let both grow together until the harvest. At that time I will tell the harvesters: "first collect the weeds and tie them in bundles to be burned; then gather the wheat and bring it into my barn."'

Lord of the Harvest
Knows what we need

He sends out laborers
To harvest a seed

Whatever they find
Let it grow there

"I will separate
The wheat from the tare
All in due season
The fullness of time
Each and everyday
Cultivation is mine"

Touch everyone, Lord
Thresh our Spirit with-in

Start with me, Lord
We're none without sin.

It's My Time

Isaiah 40:29-31 NIV

He gives strength to the weary and increases the power of the weak. Even youths grow tired and weary, and young men stumble and fall; but those who hope in the LORD will renew their strength. They will soar on wings like eagles; they will run and not grow weary, they will walk and not be faint.

It's my time to stop and thank You
For my life Lord, with gratitude
Forgive me for the years I spent
Being ungrateful and so rude

You are a loving, faithful and forgiving God
That knows where every moment went
Yet your hand was upon me, even then
Thank You Lord, nothing is by accident

What can I say, except I'm grateful
That you placed so much value on me
You held, nurtured and watched me grow
From a sapling into a strong rooted tree

Often times I craved friend's blessings
And their seeming prosperity
It was a chasing of the wind, Lord
Not your plan for my destiny

Thank You for bringing it all together
In Your time-with strength and peace
As I trust and submit to your will
Sharing truth in Love, has increased

Thanks for yesterday, today and tomorrow
Cradled in the palm of your right hand
For you a thousand years is as one day
All creation obeys your command

Thank You for revelation knowledge
And lovingly empowering me
It's my time to be grounded and rooted
In the things of God: I'm grateful, eternally

Keeper Of A Caged Bird

Psalm 32:1-2 NIV

Blessed is he whose transgressions are forgiven, whose sins are covered. Blessed is the man whose sin the LORD does not count against him and in whose spirit is no deceit.

Energy is ultimately sapped
Mind is confused and trapped
Hope is lost and capped

Wings clipped
Beak tipped

Life is bored
Intentions ignored
Anger outpoured
Usefulness stored

Heart bleeding
Body needing

What's left to do
Everything's meaningless for you
Is anything in life true
Is anything under the sun new

Out of his cage he tore
Not to be kept anymore

Keeper of a caged bird, can't you see
This caged bird only lives to be free

Caged bird go . . . in abundant love and peace
Find your destiny in living until life is ceased

Lord, have mercy on us all!

Law And Spirit

Micah 6:8 NIV

He has showed you, O man, what is good. And what does the LORD
require of you?
To act justly and to love mercy and to walk humbly with your God

Change me with love—Change me in love
With love I can bear anything
With love I can bear everything
Anything-everything else is veiled
Far, far from my peace

Selah!

Listen

Philippians 3:13-16 NIV

Brothers, I do not consider myself yet to have taken hold of it. But one thing I do: Forgetting what is behind and straining toward what is ahead, press on toward the goal to win the prize for which God has called me heavenward in Christ Jesus. All of us who are mature should take such a view of things. And if on some point you think different: That too God will make clear to you. Only let us live up to what we have already attained.

I have learned one thing
That I must not do
Interfere with the plan
The Lord has for you

My greatest hope and
To The Lord I pray
As I follow my vision
Do not block your way

We all have a part
In God's perfect plan
Listen;
God reveals Himself in
Visions and dreams to man

Don't follow your emotions,
By what I say or do
Just pursue the plan
God has called you to

It's not my intention
To stand in your way
Everything's set in order
When we stand and pray

God's working thru us
His Eternal Plan
That's why He is God
And we are called man

Living My Song

Romans 1:19 AMP

For that which is known about God is evident to them and made plain in their inner consciousness, because God [Himself] has shown it to them.

Don't have much to offer
A Friend with everything
But-remind you of the Song
That only YOU can sing

We're all under construction
Grace covers every sin
Love is a compelling light
Displaying that gift with-in

Let no obstacle make you say
I'll do it tomorrow-not today
Hope and opportunity clears the way
To conquer those thoughts and sail away

You've got it, you can do it—it's a beautiful thing
No one else can complete it—it's your song to sing
Be enlightened and empowered—give Honor to God
Like Aaron before his enemy—throw down your rod

Shout:
My heart's open and my mind is free
To sing my song and finally, just be
Everything My Lord expects of me

My song to sing
My bell to ring
My flower to smell
My story to tell
Let my light shine
And finally, be
Love and Peace . . . Confidently!

Creations waiting, now humbly say "Thank God for all I'll encounter today!!!"

When your mind is free—you are free indeed

Don't let anyone steal your light and life purpose. Invite them to live their own life song—God is good he made room for us all in His garden and at his table.
Every difference is an asset to compliment and complete you.

Lord of the Harvest

Luke 10:2 NIV

He told them, "The harvest is plentiful, but the workers are few. Ask the Lord of the harvest, therefore, to send out workers into his harvest field.

I am Your vessel
Filled with Your Spirit
And Your Spirit knows
Lord, Your Spirit knows

Lord of the harvest
Knows what we need
He sends out laborers
To sow His seed
Water it with love
Much tender care
He returns a harvest
Our storehouse can't bear

Everything I have
Everything I do
Everything I need Lord
Comes from You
I am so thankful
To bear Your Spirit
Where Your Spirit goes
Every seed grows

You gave your life
Took full control
You won the battle
For spirit and soul
Lord of the harvest
Knows what we need
There's victory-victory
In every seed!

Love And Obey

Matthew 28:19-20 NIV

"Therefore go and make disciples of all nations, baptizing them in the name of the Father and of the Son and of the Holy Spirit, and teaching them to obey everything I have commanded you. And surely I am with you always, to the very end of the age."

Hearken unto Your word-Lord
Hasten unto Your throne
Covered in the same eternal promises
That our forefathers stood on

You have loved, directed and kept us
No matter the circumstance
Led us to lie still before you
Revealed your plan is not by chance

Lord, keep your hand upon us
Strengthen us year by year
Restore all the enemy has stolen
Bring rejoicing to every tear

Crown us with grace and glory
New mercies we receive every day
Renew a right Spirit with-in us
Always blessing the kingdom, your way

Our purpose is your unique call
You blessed the hour and the day
Remind us to share with all men
The Good-News of Your Love:
Hooray!

We live, because You live Lord

Love Is

John 13:34 NIV

**"A new command I give you: Love one another as I have loved you,
So you must Love on another."**

*Love does have a perfect plan
Love includes every man*

*You can't give all your love away
Love is renewed everyday*

Love is life

Love gives life

*Love is truth that is free
I'll let Love speak for me*

Amen!

Manifesting Power

John 17:24-26 NIV

"Father, I want those you have given me to be with me where I am, and to see my glory, the glory you have given me because you loved me before the creation of the world. "Righteous Father, though the world does not know you, I know you, and they know that you have sent me. I have made you known to them, and will continue to make you Known, In order that the love you have for me may be in them and that I myself may be in them."

By your power Lord, by your might
By Your will, everything's made right
The battles over, we've won the fight
Overcame darkness, walking in the light

You've destroyed the enemy with Your Sovereign hand
And empowered the warriors with faith to stand
Proclaiming peace and love, for guilt and shame
Declaring eternal life, in Jesus Name

Low places are exalted, mountains are made low
Rough places smooth, everywhere we go
Stand in light of truth, and speak what we know
The bearer of good news, with seeds to sow

We see from the cross, with renewed authority
Strength to break the back of the enemy
Blind eyes are opened and men see they're free
To pursue their purpose and destiny

Thank You for Your blood and saving power
For Your amazing grace, every hour
Most Holy, Merciful and Worthy Lord
Manifest Your Love
Manifest Your Love
Manifest Your Love—in us on one accord

Mighty Warrior

Matthew 9:37 NIV

Then he said to his disciples, "The harvest is plentiful but the workers are few."

Harvest fields are ripe
Grain is bending gold
Workers are few
Soldiers won't do as told

Brothers and sisters are dying
Fading out of sight
Souls are not turning to God
Soldiers will not fight

On your day of reckoning
Ought not be said of you
All you needed was in your possession
But you failed to follow through

You are blessed with this chance
To turn that fate around
Love pierces the core of hearts
Gilead's balm has been found

Harvest fields are ripe
Grain is bending gold
God needs mighty warriors
To fight for all hungry souls

Victorious and powerful God
Mightiest warrior of all
Placed victory inside of you
Long before He called

It's time to make that decision
Acknowledge truth-cry if you must
The Holy Spirit of God
Knows warriors He can trust

Harvest fields are ripe
Grain is bending gold
Everywhere you look
There are precious, hungry souls

Harvest fields are ripe
Grain is bending gold
God planted you mighty warrior
To lead them back into the fold

Amen!

My Lord

2ⁿᵈ Corr.1:3-4 NIV

Praise be to the God and Father of our Lord Jesus Christ, the Father
of Compassion And the God of all comfort, who comforts us in all our
troubles, so that we can comfort Those in any trouble with the comfort we
ourselves have received from God.

Calmed the torrential waters
Quieted the raging sea
Stilled the agonizing fear
And confusion inside of me

God spoke "peace", so I listened
Love filled my soul and mind
"Fear not, for all is forgiven
And you are eternally Mine"

Now I live to praise my Jesus
The Lord and Redeemer of my life
He continually strengthens and keeps me
In truth, from misery and strife

I trust you eternally and forever
That's how long I'll exalt You, My Lord
I've joined your host of angels
Singing Hosanna on one accord

Only you are worthy Master
Of the honor and the praise
You are The King of Glory
And you keep my head upraised

Thank You Sovereign Lord for all that you are,
In Jesus Name

Amen!

My Sister

Isaiah 55:10-11 NIV

As the rain and the snow come down from heaven, and do not return to it without watering the earth and making it bud and flourish, so that it yields seed for the sower and bread for the eater, so is my word that goes out from my mouth: It will not return to me empty, but will accomplish what I desire and achieve the purpose for which I sent it.

As the days and seasons go by
You will realize more and more
What the Lord is saying to you
And everything He has in store

You're a blessed and wonderful mother
And you are a great and faithful friend
God knows every detail of your journey
He promises victory in the end

Proceed and follow your inner-peace
Praise Jesus radically in all you do
Don't take any blessings for granted

Because:
God cultivates seeds to make strong trees
So His Light and Love can shine through

Love and Hugs
Today and always,

Thank God for You,
Amen!

Neighbor

James 1:22-25 NIV

Do not merely listen to the word, and so deceive yourselves. Do what it says. Anyone who listens to the word but does not do what it says is like someone who looks At his face in a mirror and, after looking at himself, goes away and immediately forgets what he looks like.

What did he do or where did he go
What is my motive for wanting to know

What did he say or how much did he get
Once I know what will I do with it

Where are they going or where have they been
Is your mind flowing with blessings, my friend

Don't say it's not my fault or I really don't care
Attitudes like these reject and beware

We must not judge our brothers level of sin
We have no Heaven or Hell to put him in

Be a doer of the Word, written in God's Book
Truth reflects in the mirror, if we only look

Amen!

We can do all things as Christ Jesus, strengthens us.

No Chains Holding Me

John 8:31-32 NIV

**To the Jews who had believed him, Jesus said, "If you hold to my teaching,
you are really my disciples. Then you will know the truth,
and the truth will set you free."**

*We are moving around in this physical world
Thinking that we are free*

*But when we are bound-up in our mind
We are locked-up mentally*

*Do you have a plan to free yourself
Without The Lord you'll stay locked-in*

*Looking in the mirror from the other side
Is a lonesome place, my friend*

*If you want to live in love and peace
To conquer life mentally*

Just examine every thought in truth
Beloved: truth will set you free

Beloved, whom the Son has set free, is free indeed.

We serve an awesome God
He abolishes every wall
He is always with us
He hears us when we call
Builds bridges over troubles of life
Gives victory over misery and strife
His arms are always open
We needn't fret or despair
His Spirit leads us to peace inside
Lord loves us and He Cares

Amen!

Noises

Jeremiah 9:20 *NIV*

Now, O women, hear the word of the LORD;
open your ears to the words of his mouth.
Teach your daughters how to wail; teach one another a lament.

Lord:

What in the world
Is this world coming to
Where are the wailing women
And what should they do

Holy Spirit, speak
I desire to hear from you
Every other voice be silent
Because I command you to

Take charge of every thought
Take control of my ear
The voice of a stranger
I will not hear

I know we shouldn't be anxious
Nor should we walk in fear
Help us be strong for others
That we hold so dear

Amen!

Not Me

Acts 19:11 NIV

God did extraordinary miracles through Paul

Lord, Your Faithfulness protects,
My lack of faith in you
Your Super covers my natural
Your authority brings me through

My Lord, You fed the multitudes
You parted the Red Sea
You raised Lazarus
You died for me

You hold all power
Your Name is Grace
We share a covenant anointing
Endless time and space

Your super covering my natural
Brings forth miracles everyday
Now that I know it's not me
Merciful Lord, have your way

In Jesus Name,

Amen!

Not One

Genesis 22:13 NIV

Abraham looked up and there in a thicket he saw a ram caught by its horns.
He went over and took the ram and sacrificed it as a
burnt offering Instead of his son.

Lord, I'm not always listening
But you always teach
What's that saying about those souls
You created me to reach

Thank you Lord of the harvest
You love us even when we stray
Gently guide us to the ram in the thicket
That you have safely tucked away

Amen!

Nothing

Matthew *16:16 NIV*

Simon Peter answered, "You are the Christ, the Son of the living God."

Anything I call You, Lord
Anything I will do
Anything I can imagine
Won't fully describe You

You are God, My Father
And my faithful Friend
Royal High Priest, forever
You forgave all my sins

You are my redeemer
And my strong tower too
You win every battle
I give over to you

You're Alpha and Omega
Created earth with me in mind
If I search all eternity
Words are light years behind

Amen!

Peace in the Storm

Mark 4: 39-40 NIV

He got up, rebuked the wind and said to the waves, "Quiet! Be still!"
Then the wind died down and it was completely calm. He said to his
disciples, "Why are you so afraid? Do you still have no faith?"

Some things I ponder in my heart
Some things I quickly throw away
Some things I speak to others about
But not before I pray

Every thought that comes from My Lord
Every word that's spoken too
Every intention of God's heart
Is reconciling Himself to you

Take no thought unto yourself
That's not The Masters Will
The storms and waves must obey
When He says Peace be still

He is the Master of the seas
The mountain and valley too
Wherever you find yourself
He is right in there with you

Rest in the valley with comfort
Ride the waves with peace
Until the Captain of your life
Tells the storm to cease

Everything has a purpose
Every season-there's a plan
Thank God you're not alone
You're in His Sovereign hand

Don't think you are forgotten
Don't fear you are thrown away
Master is rearranging things
Tell the flesh to obey

You're wonderfully made in his image
Highly favored with authority
Pray what to ponder in your heart
And from every lie be free

In Jesus Name,
Amen!

Pick Up The Pieces

Galatians 5:22-26 NIV

But the fruit of the Spirit is love, joy, peace, patience, kindness, goodness, faithfulness, Gentleness and self-control. Against such things there is no law. Those who belong to Christ Jesus have crucified the sinful nature with its passions and desires. Since we live by the Spirit, let us keep in step with the Spirit. Let us not become conceited, provoking and envying each other.

There's a piece of my heart right there before you
Separate-but, longing to be embraced and a part of

Listen to my silent screams, I need you desperately
Please show compassion—stop, let's share true Love

Love that listens beyond the words I've spoken
Love that transforms the inmost heart of things

Love that patiently binds-up and cancels mental anguish
Breaks through despair: loose the song my heart sings

Love that will join in and encourage my rhyme and melody
Even when that rhyme makes no sense at all

Love that is long-suffering with understanding
Faithful Love that will be there, just because

I know as my heart is enriched and strengthened
And those separate pieces are made whole again

I will joyfully share that same True Love mending
The silent screams I discern in my fellowman.

Thank you Lord for Christ Jesus . . . who is LOVE!!!

Amen!

Power

Ephesians 6:11 NIV

Put on the full armor of God so that you can take your stand against the devil's schemes.

Sometimes, when I pray, and pray, and pray
I realize, that the adversary is never going away

I feel confusion, fear and anger, tear my spirit down
My joy, peace and love are stifled and bound

When I asked My Lord; "what should I say or do
I need confidence right now, and strength from You"

"Speak to that mountain" is the reply that I heard
"Use sanctified power and authority in every word"

"Fear and mind control has come to an end
You see every trick and scheme, and no longer bend"

Declare:
"My chains are broken and I am completely free
By Eternal God, who has Sovereign Authority
The Holy Spirit lives in all-and is protecting me
I have everything I need, from the Blessed Trinity."

"Remind him the light has pierced the darkness and God's in control
Rest in your armor beloved, cause your names on Heavens roll"

Amen!

Priceless

Psalm *103:12 NLT*

He has removed our sins as far from us as the east is from the west.

Why am I trying so hard to be someone I'm not
Why am I again seeking forgiveness for things that
You've already forgot

Maybe I've not allowed myself to focus on truth
And enlighten my mind with thoughts of Love
Remembering who I am to you

Peaceful in both: Your embrace-or a loving shove

The question doesn't define me: The answer does
I am who I am today, because of whom I was

Every melancholy moment
Every urge to act, right now
Every unharnessed thought
Every furrowed brow

Every scurried action
Every forlorn sigh
Every intention of my heart
Every urge to cry

They are all priceless to You, Lord!!!

God created both the adversary and me—to make me better

Reach Out, To You

Romans 8:27-28 NIV

And he who searches our hearts knows the mind of the Spirit, because the Spirit intercedes for the saints in accordance with God's will. And we know that in all things God works for the good of those who love him, who have been called according to his purpose.

*Yes, you are here
But, God knows your name*

*Rebuke the shame
And love just the same*

*Release the pain
Of seeking riches and fame*

*Forgive your brother
He's not to blame*

*You're never alone
God knows your name*

Beloved:

*"Tears are stored in a bottle
They are safely put away*

*I know everything about you
And hear you when you pray*

*You are already forgiven
Give Me your burdens today"*

Redeemer

2 Corinthians 12:9 NIV

But he said to me, "My grace is sufficient for you, for my power is made perfect in weakness." Therefore I will boast all the more gladly about my weaknesses, so that Christ's power may rest on me.

Hello Lord
It's me! Yes it's me again
Standing here all alone
In need of a true friend

Hello Lord
Please help me even though
I've waited much too long
And have no place left to go

Make it right: Make it right, again

Hello Lord
Supplier of Good seeds to sow
My spirits crying out for truth
Tell me what I need to know

Hello Lord
I'm trying hard to understand
Don't know what else to do
Solid ground is now sinking sand

Make it right: Make it right Lord, again

Hello Lord
I confess my love for You
You've empowered me to hope
And revealed true love too

Hello Lord
Now I fully understand
Your bloods already redeemed me
Righteous-Redeemer of every man
It's all right: It's all right Lord, again

Amen!

Right Now, Lord

1 Thessalonians 5:9 NIV

**For God did not appoint us to suffer wrath but to receive salvation
through our Lord Jesus Christ.**

*No more stooping over
I am standing tall*

*No more standing still
I am moving forward*

*No more receiving circumstances
I am changing the atmosphere*

*No more looking at the cross
I am looking from the cross*

*Our Savior lives and
I have Eternal Victory*

Amen!

Rightful Place

Matthew 18:20 NIV

"For where two or three come together in my name, there am I with them"

Just got a handle on all your problems, they're nestled in just right
And you are confronted with another problem that disturbs you all night

You don't know what to do with it and you're trying even harder not to care
Hopefully, this problem will fit with the others, and still have room to spare

Remember, God is your source: Decide not to fear, moan and whine
God has already made provision for this problem, to nestle in just fine

I recall times I walked in fear, or I would scream and shout
Thanks Lord for grace and mercy: You always work things out

This problem will fit where you say fit, and go where you say go
I'm grateful you're ever—present: In due season you let me know

You could tell me the door is closed and go back where I belong
Instead you say "my child you are forgiven, even though you were wrong"

You could also tell me to be quiet: I'm hearing no more problems today
Instead you lend an attentive ear and console me every time I pray

When I think about the goodness of Jesus, and all He does for me
I can't complain about my problems, no matter how big they seem to be

Sometimes I take my eyes off of Jesus and problems press down on me
I become difficult and outright testy; but that's not who I desire to be

I desire to say-God is Good and I can handle everything that comes my way
With a smile-I'd like to say God be with you, the rest of this beautiful day

Only when I take my eyes off Jesus, does our relationship fall out of grace
Problems come and situations change, but with Jesus they nestle into place

Love conquers; forgiveness is commonplace, as we seek The Masters face
So please don't get angry, just pray with me to return to our rightful place

Bless God—Bless God,
Amen!

Safe In His Arms

Ephesians 4:30 NIV

And do not grieve the Holy Spirit of God, with whom you were sealed for the day of redemption.

Lord God Almighty
Holy and Righteous
Creator of earth and all men

Lord God Almighty
Holy and Righteous
Redeemer and Restorer of sin

You already know Him
You already feel Him
He already dwells with-in

Lord God Almighty
Holy and Righteous
He desires to be your best friend

You already know Him
You already feel Him
He already dwells with-in

Just let Him comfort
Love and heal you
Give you peace that no one else can
Peace that no one else can

Amen!

Saved

Psalm 91:14-16 NIV

"Because he loves me," says the LORD, "I will rescue him;
I will protect him, for he acknowledges my name.
He will call on me, and I will answer him; I will be with him in trouble,
I will deliver him and honor him.
With long life I will satisfy him and show him my salvation."

Thank you Lord for loving her from the cradle to her earthly end
You taught her how to be a loving mother, daughter and a friend

There were times she would have given up: I'd hear her call on you
A joyous smile would come on her face; like she knew just what to do

Saying child don't worry talk to Jesus, from that secret place with-in
Jesus knows all about it and He Loves you anyway, even in your sin

She'd often break out in songs of praise and didn't care who would hear
Heaviness in the air would change and bring joy into the atmosphere

Humbly complete her tasks whether hosting, cleaning toilets or the floor
I'd hear her gathering the things she'd need and quietly close the door

When I acted out she wouldn't say a word: just give a certain look
Merciful Lord, back then I knew a certain look was all it took

I remember that old chair where she would sit quietly holding me
Her smell, her hair, her warm embrace, humming songs of Jubilee

I'm thankful for our time together; sharing life, love and legacy
Shared your earthly angel for a season, now she's an angel for eternity

Mom I pray my children will see in my life, half what I saw in you
They'll love The Lord: value our season and say I'm an angel too!

Thank you for your dwelling place Most High God,

Amen!

Shall Be

John 10:5 NIV

But they will never follow a stranger; in fact, they will run away from him because they do not recognize a stranger's voice."

Dear Lord:

Speak to my shall be
From afar or from near
My spirit does know your voice
A stranger I will not hear

Everything that I am
Everything that I do
Everything that I shall be
I offer back to you

Today and everyday in Jesus Name,

Amen!

Spoken Vision

Habakkuk *2:2-3 NIV*

**Then the LORD replied: "Write down the revelation
and make it plain on tablets so that a herald may run with it."**

Speak the Word Lord, make it plain
Sum it up in Jesus Name

Wherever I go, whatever I do
Must be blessed and led by you

Write the vision on my heart
This experience won't depart

Write the vision in my spirit
All men will be drawn near it

Write the vision in my hands
They will carry out your plans

Write the vision in my mind
With the power to loose and bind

Write the vision Lord, right away
Souls crying out, night and day

Speak the Word that compels me
To inform every man they're already free

Speak the Word head to feet
Overflowing from the Mercy Seat

Write the vision there's no lack
Seal the covenant, no turning back

All authority comes from You, Majesty:
In Jesus Name,

Amen!

Still

Psalm 46:1-3 NIV

God is our refuge and strength, an ever-present help in trouble. Therefore we will not fear Though the earth give way and the mountains fall into the heart of the sea, Though its waters roar and foam and the mountains quake with their surging.

The Lord is in His tabernacle
He is on His Holy hill
He surrounds us with His goodness
If only we would keep still

He wants our eyes to be opened
With faith, we're able to see
He's with us in the valley, or mountain
Wherever we may be

Keep still and hear the promises
To know God's will for you
Walk in the fullness of His blessings
Prosper in all that you do

The Lord is in His tabernacle
It's His pleasure, and His will
To love, strengthen and encourage us
If only we would keep still

Speak to our hearts, Lord Jesus
Anoint us to do your will
As we lift our voices in your tabernacle
And, our hope to Your Holy hill

Holy Spirit, come: Empower us,
To be ever-faithful and show
Jesus blood makes us more than conquerors
To share abundant life, everywhere we go

The Lord is in His tabernacle
He is on His Holy hill
His Covenant is Everlasting to Everlasting
HE IS FAITHFUL—STILL

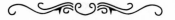

Surrender

Zechariah 13:9 NIV

"This third I will put into the fire; I will refine them
like silver and test them like gold.
They will call on my name and I will answer them; I will say,
'They are my people,'
And they will say, 'The LORD is our God.'"

Come Lord, the Potter: I am your mold
Purge and refine me: Till I'm pure gold

I feel you tugging at my hearts door
Leading me to your threshing floor

Your touch dear Lord is oh, so sweet
Bless me to bless, everyone I meet
Bless me to bless, everyone I meet

In Jesus Mighty Name,

Amen!

The Angel That Feels Me

Ephesians 6:2-3 NIV

Honor your father and mother" which is the first commandment
with a promise "so that it may go well with you and that you
may enjoy long life on the earth."

I don't have to worry about a dress, food or shoe
You take care of all that, and darling I thank you

You wash my face-you clean my hands
And when I don't talk, you understand

You keep the Faith: You stroke my hair
I see you smile, as you utter a prayer

No matter what chore you have to do
Your peaceful Spirit says: I LOVE YOU

Time with me is the highlight of your day
I see that sad look when you must go away

Squeeze of your hand and warm embrace
Puts time in a bottle: We share one space

At times it might appear as if I don't care
I'm thanking God, and whispering a prayer

For my Beloved Angel and friend, I know
He sent you to feel me Daughter: Long ago

I love you for all that you do
I thank God for sending you

Your efforts are not in vain: God cares all about you

AMEN!

The Beloved

Ephesians *1:5-6 NIV*

He predestined us for adoption to son ship through Jesus Christ, In accordance with his pleasure and will—to the praise of his glorious grace, Which he has freely given us in the One he loves.

This son is not everything I desire him to be
Thank God his destiny doesn't rest on me

LORD:

Compel me to cast every worry onto you
Free me to focus on what I am called to do

Help me perfect my assignment everyday
To inspire, to encourage, and listen as I pray

You created this child for your perfect will
Reveal your strategy, cause me to keep still

We trust you Dear Lord, let Your will be done
Grant us love and peace, he's Your Beloved son

You protect your own
You perfect your own

Thank You Majesty for new grace and mercy everyday

In Jesus Name,

Amen!

The Bridegroom Cometh

Matthew 25:10 NIV

"But while they were on their way to buy the oil, the bridegroom arrived.
The virgins who were ready went in with him to the wedding banquet.
And the door was shut.

Lord, where are all of the wailing women
Where did they all go

I am standing here by myself
As if you did not know

Did they get tired of standing
Lose faith and go back home

Maybe they forgot their assignment
And their mind started to roam

Maybe they went out to buy more oil
Or their wick needs a light

Lord, if I am in this battle all alone
How can we win this fight

Beloved:

"Don't worry about those women
Wherever they might be
I have legions praying right now
Doing work you cannot see
Stay here and keep on praying
Faithfully watch—till you hear from Me"

Amen!

The Enemy Within

John *3:16 NIV*

"For God so loved the world that he gave his one and only Son, that whoever believes in him shall not perish but have eternal life."

Question is-are you fighting the right fight
Standing up for Jesus both day and night
Are you convinced that love is the way
Persist in truth, regardless what men say

Christ stayed on the cross for you and me
Created hope in truth; for eternal liberty
He opened our eyes to every mystery
And lifted our burdens, to embrace unity

I know it's hard and sometimes it's tough
What you are enduring is more than enough
Be encouraged-hold on, in Jesus Mighty Name
He knows who you are and He feels your pain

There are no heartaches The Lord can't ease
There is no desire that He can't please
He created the universe, creation and man
Every sin is forgiven, that's His perfect plan

Reject secret lies and torment that grip your heart
Praise Jesus for His Love anytime anguish starts
Refuse deceit the enemy whispers in your ear
Creating doubt, confusion, anger and fear

It really doesn't matter what he whispers and say
He will stop lying and leave, when you boldly pray
Thank God for mercy, and praise Him for grace
For a joy-filled spirit, and a smile on your face

The power of The Holy Spirit gives you authority
Yes, you're fighting the right fight for Victory
The mind is a battlefield for every man
But the Blood of Jesus gives us power to stand

Reject the victim mentality
You are redeemed, healed and free
Say "no more lies whispered to me
Jesus blood gives me authority
To live in Blessed Victory"
Amen!

The Family

Ephesians 1:5-6 NIV

He predestined us for adoption to son ship through Jesus Christ, in accordance with his pleasure and will—to the praise of his glorious grace, which he has freely given us in the One he loves.

CHRIST JESUS,

Shed His Holy Blood for me
On the cross, on the cross at Calvary
My chains are broken and I'm set free
No longer a servant, I'm family

Washed in His Blood: Washed in His Blood
My chains are broken, I'm set free
Washed in His Blood: Washed in His Blood
I'm in, I'm in the Family

Come Holy Spirit, come Holy Spirit
Come touch and reveal yourself to me
Come Holy Spirit, come Holy Spirit
I yield all to the Trinity

Come Holy Spirit, come Holy Spirit
Fresh Grace and Anointing, empower me
Lift me high above principalities
Thank You Christ Jesus, for victory

Washed in His Blood: Washed in His Blood
My chains are broken, I'm set free
Washed in His Blood: Washed in His Blood
I'm in, I'm in The Family

Washed in His Blood: Washed in His Blood
Spirit of the Living God flows thru me
Bearing much fruit with power, you see

I'm no longer a servant
I'm a child of The King
Chosen and caught-up
Forgiven and washed clean
Redeemed in His Blood
I have all of the privileges'
All of the promises
I'm in, I'm in The Family

Amen!

The Gift Of Grace

1 Corinthians 12:11 NIV

**All these are the work of one and the same Spirit,
and he distributes them to each one, just as he determines.**

*You are gift
A precious gift
The Lord's Spirit within you*

*You bring a gift
A transforming gift
Loving kindness inside of you*

*You take the gift
You make the gift
A cup the Anointing flows thru
The faithful gift within you
The perfect gift inside of you*

The gift is Holy-Holy
The gift is Righteous-Righteous
The gift is Mighty-Mighty
The gift will bless you-Bless you
Just submit, praise and commit to
The faithful gift within you
The precious gift inside of you

Take care how you present me
Trust me to break souls free
Love Me I am Holy-Holy
Keep Me I am Mighty-Mighty
Submit, praise and commit to
The Perfect gift inside of you

My Peace covers you in all that you do!

The Grace Of God

2 Corinthians 12:9 NIV

But he said to me, "My grace is sufficient for you, for my power is made perfect in weakness." Therefore I will boast all the more gladly about my weaknesses, so that Christ's power may rest on me.

Keep doing what you are anointed to do
Until the bell tolls for you

Miracles and signs occur, everyday
When yielded vessels trust God and obey

If the bell tolls for family, or friends
The veil is torn, Christ took our sin

Until that bell rings, for your enemies
Pray their eyes be opened and they might see

Don't let any trials, or their grim face
Move you from The Glory, of God's Grace

Don't get weary for the day or the hour
God does not lie: He has resurrection power

God blessed and loves every hair on your head
He knows every thought, deed and word you've said

When your journey on the road gets tough
Remember, you serve a God of more than enough

With hope in Glory: A crown waiting for you
Stay strong in the Lord there's much work to do

Speak to the four winds today, and know
Our generation's inheritance, will grow

The day that Glorious bell, tolls for you
God's all-sufficient Grace will carry you through!

Proclaim victory in Spirit and in truth for the kingdom,
Amen!

The Promise

Genesis 28:15 NIV

**I am with you and will watch over you wherever you go,
and I will bring you back to this land. I will not leave you until
I have done what I have promised you."**

*Jesus, wonderful Counselor, Jesus comforter and Friend
Jesus, mighty Warrior, He is with you, until the end*

*Jesus, Lord of Lords, Jesus, Prince of peace
Jesus, Great Intercessor, Praising you will never cease*

*Call Him in the morning
Call Him in the midnight hour
Call Him anytime
You need His Sovereign power
Thank Him for His Blessings
Thank Him for His Grace
Thank Him for His Peace
And comforting embrace
Praise Him for the small things
Praise Him wherever you go
Praise Him in the Spirit of Truth
Expect your love to grow
Depend on Him like your Father
Call Him like your Friend
With a passion for His Spirit
Walk in Victory till the end*

Jesus, Wonderful Counselor, Jesus, comforter and Friend
Jesus Mighty Warrior, He is with you, until the end

Jesus, Lord of Lords, Jesus, Prince of Peace
Jesus, Great Intercessor, Praising you will never cease

This Battle

2 Chronicles 20:15 NIV

He said: "Listen, King Jehoshaphat and all who live in Judah and Jerusalem! This is what the LORD says to you: 'Do not be afraid or discouraged because of this vast army: For the battle is not yours, but God's."

Concern yourself more with
How you will rise

Than your concern for
Your enemies' demise;

For the Lord is with thee

Amen!

Pray to love and trust truth

This Time

Psalm 50:12 NIV

If I were hungry I would not tell you,
for the world is mine, and all that is in it.

Oh Lord, Great Jehovah
I am wholly Thine
To You, I surrender
What I thought was mine
All power and authority
Is in Your Mighty hand
Creator of every man
And every grain of sand

You are the sunshine
That breaks thru the rain
You are overcoming joy
In the midst of my pain
And in my weakness
I'm strengthened to know
You are pruning Dear Lord
You're helping me to grow

This time I give you
All of my burdens
All of my fears
All of my doubts
All of my tears
This time, this time,
Not like the last time
This time,
I surrender all to you

This time I give You
All of those pretenses
For all of those years
And every hurt Lord
That always reappears

This time,
Because I'm nothing without you
This time
I surrender all to you

Thoughts For You

Jeremiah 29:11 NIV

"For I know the plans I have for you," declares the LORD, "plans to prosper you and not to harm you, plans to give you hope and a future."

To live and not die
To laugh and not cry
To succeed and not fail
The head—not the tail

To bless and not curse
For better or for worse
To stand and not fall
To stay on the wall

See in Spirit and know
What seeds you should sow
To walk in lovely peace
Your joy will never cease

To be happy and not sad
Forgiving heart that's glad
To pray in The Spirit and obey
Walk in victory everyday

A Royal Priest God can send
To intercede for a friend
Today and everyday,

In Jesus Name,

Amen!

Threshing Floor Of God's Heart

Leviticus 26:5 NIV

**Your threshing will continue until grape harvest, the grape harvest will
continue until planting, And you will eat all the food you want,
and live in safety in your land.**

*Lord God, You desire more of me
Touch and heal the core of me*

*Inside of me is opened wide
You see the hurts, fear and pride
From you creator, I cannot hide
Truth transforms, so come reside
Take over Lord, don't pick a side*

*Before I came to this oil of pressing
Before I came to this floor of threshing
I thought I knew of Gods true blessings*

*I lacked real Faith, Love and Understanding
Your light of Truth was too demanding
So I existed on life that fate was handing*

Now I know without a doubt
Lord God, You make the rocks cry out
Broken, yet strengthened, I proceed in Love
Peaceful in your hug or gentle shove

Proclaiming as I'm led what The Spirit commands
All men awaken to Truth, and Stand
God of everything that I truly need
You are glorified thru every seed

Amen!

Today

Hebrews 4:7 NIV

**Therefore God again set a certain day, calling it today . . .
"Today, if you hear his voice, do not harden your hearts."**

Today is the day
Now is the time
This is the place
I am the one

Prayer is my key
Love is my guide
Praise is my venue
Obedience is my marker

Wisdom is my badge
Truth is my shield
Grace is my power
God is my source

Thank you for today, Lord

I am moving forward as a conqueror,
Today

Everlasting Messiah!

Truth Is

James 1:21 NIV

Therefore, get rid of all moral filth and the evil that is so prevalent and humbly accept the word planted in you, which can save you.

This battle ain't bout stuff and thangs
This battle's all bout man
Trials and tests are to strengthen us
And enable us to stand

This battles not bout happiness
In thangs we touch and see
It's all bout the joy we share
The power-knowing we're free

We all are tested everyday
The young and the old
The battles all bout Jesus Love

TRUTH IS

The battles all bout souls!

Victory At Every Level

Philippians 3:14 NIV

**I press on toward the goal to win the prize for which
God has called me heavenward In Christ Jesus.**

*There's signs and wonders inside of you
Seek and pray what God wants you to do*

*Tell that old flesh to go and take a seat
It's not about you: It's about those you meet*

*Signs are not yours to pick and choose
You store The Holy Spirit for God to use*

*Stir-up and ignite that gift right now
There are seeds to plant, and fields to plow*

*Kingdom suffers violence, you are a source
Father God can trust to take back by force*

At every level, there's surely a test
Blessings with authority, and seasons of rest

Paul said it so clearly, one thing he must do
Press towards the mark he's called unto

After passing each test he could look and find
Much signs and wonders, he had left behind

Holy Spirit come, and have Your way
Flesh you are defeated, today

Thank You for the work of The Holy Spirit, Mighty God

Amen!

Winners

Isaiah 45:6-7 KJV

That they may know from the rising of the sun, and from the west.
That there is none beside me: I am the LORD, and there is none else.
I form the light, and create darkness: I make peace, and create evil:
I the LORD do all these things.

Losers win by leaping onto the back of others.
Losers ride the foundation that winners build.
Winners, stay awake!!!

You can't stop them from hating on you
But, don't let them get into your head
Every time they tell you what they think
Tell them what your God said:

"You are the Apple of My Eye
I Love you the way you are
Now, love yourself with confidence
And every wound become a scar

You are a winner because I say so
I gave that vision to you
I placed the adversary in your path
And strength to make it thru

I see everything you're doing
I know everything they say
Let every scar speak for itself
Tell them, I'm not hearing you today

If your greatest feat is hating on me
And your life's purpose is fulfilled
I thank God for you my brother
And I have erased all ill-will.

Words

Psalm 19:14 NIV

May the words of my mouth and the meditation of my heart be pleasing in your sight, O LORD, my Rock and my Redeemer

Some words come, some words go
Some words are hidden, some words show
Some words I don't, some I know
Some words kill, but some grow

Not one word going from you
Is ever hidden, numerous or few
They're all the same
Glorious-Victorious
They're all true
Majesty!

Take every word Lord, no matter the sound
Use it for Your Glory, turn it around
Bless every words purpose and destiny
For love and peace, break our hearts free

To faithfully live in unity
Good and merciful God, start with me

In Jesus Name,
Amen!

You Did Not Choose Me- I Chose You

John 15:16-17 NIV

"You did not choose me, but I chose you and appointed you to go and bear fruit: Fruit that will last. Then the Father will give you whatever you ask in my name. This is my command: Love each other . . ."

My Beloved:

I called you and established you to love Me
I see you and I know your ways

Nothing is hidden:

That which was buried, is uncovered
That which was dark, is exposed to light
That which was broken, is restored
That which was severed, is reconciled

That which was dead, shall live
The breech is repaired
The lost one, has been found

Thank You Mighty God; praise unto high Heaven:

Worship The King, Worship The King
Lift every voice, Worship The King
Come on and praise, everyone sing
Lift your voices, and Worship The King

Bless His Holy Name,
Amen!

Edwards Brothers Malloy
Thorofare, NJ USA
July 17, 2013